Goodbye Mom

A TODDLER PREP™ BOOK

Ready
SetPrep

About Toddler Prep™ Books

The best way to prepare a child for any new experience is to help them understand what to expect beforehand, according to experts. And while cute illustrations and fictional dialogue might be entertaining, little ones need a more realistic representation to fully understand and prepare for new experiences.

With Toddler Prep™ Books, a series by ReadySetPrep™, you can help your child make a clear connection between expectation and reality for all of life's exciting new firsts. Born from firsthand experience and based on research from leading developmental psychologists, the series was created by Amy and Aaron Pittman — parents of two who know (all too well) the value of preparation for toddlers.

Mom is very special. You love to be with her all the time. She makes you feel safe and happy.

You have so much fun when you're with Mom. You laugh, play games, and cuddle.

And Mom *always* takes good care of you. She loves you so much.

But sometimes you have to say goodbye to Mom - just for a little while.

You might say goodbye to her in the morning when you go to school . . .

. . . or when she has to go to work.

Sometimes you say goodbye when she has to go to the store. . .

. . .or to the gym for exercise.

But no matter where she goes, Mom *always* comes back.

There are lots of fun ways to say goodbye. You can give her a big hug and kiss. I wonder how tight you can squeeze?

Or you can give her a high five or maybe even have a secret handshake.

Then, when it's time to go, Mom says, "Goodbye. I love you! I'll see you soon."

You might feel a little sad to say goodbye to her. It's ok to feel sad. Remember, Mom *always* comes back.

If you feel sad, you can give your favorite stuffed animal a BIG hug just like you would give Mom a big hug.

17

While Mom is gone, you can do so many fun things...

You can play with your favorite toys or even draw her a picture.

You can listen to music and do a silly dance. Show me your best dance!

Sometimes you might think about Mom when she is gone. Just remember, Mom *always* comes back.

And before you know it, she is back here to see you!

When Mom comes back, you can give her a great big hug and kiss! Hooray!

And she is so excited
to hear about all the
fun things you
did. It's so nice
to be with
Mom.

Made in the USA
Coppell, TX
31 December 2024

43743716R00017